The Road Ahead:
Disarming Terrorists and dialogues with Isis et al.

By

Indana Simonde

ISBN:9781549542473

In Principio

Rehabilitation, Globalisation and Gradation within discontented structures of ideal, integrity and honour are adaptable and more recently have proven to be self-reliant and fitting current social normalisation. Empires were constructed and destroyed in the time it takes for an individual to come to maturity through perception of morals, deriving sensation and emotion from the musings of an uncomfortable idea or ideology. The concept of ideas, ideology, even concepts such as the psyche are not new conceptions. Unyet the very nature of treatment of metaphysical doubts alluded to the foundation of perceptions long held as custom or social norms.

Rights and duties are constitutional terms that refer to the very liberties and freedom we live for and by. Yet despite the failure of idealism in the realised world, the failure is not of one constitution, but every institution.

The infinitesimal universality and degree of diversification of mankind is an objective reality. As such, knowledge of all things, sensible and insensible are implanted within the psyche as cues; received or perceived and reasoned synaptic responses to a finite substance. As such they are judged and perceived notions of discursive reasoning and logic. Such reasoned and varied questions of existential substance are the basics for axioms presuppositions and theorem that challenge corporeal inequalities.

    Merely, on account of thought, the sole impetus for the formulations of questions of corporeal reality, as depicted from an objective exercise on the questions plaguing mankind. Questions of nothingness and all things spring into action by error or accident where no formal education is undertaken. This very same reality embued by science with an understanding of geological data suremises information that relates to everything from the Earth's mantle to the outermost reaches of the universe and beyond. This can be perceived by the mind of an individual to be both in existence and not in existece due to the nature and pace of modern life.

    Merely an abstraction, where the mind wonders, an idea, an axiom, a precept or presupposition, theorem or divergent train of thought can and usually does require a conclusion. Whether founded on reasoned logic or knowledge depends entirely on a honed skillset and (or) on account of any discursive reading on objective reality through acceptance of the language surrounding the axiom.

On account of the nature of the senses, hypotheses can be found to be true or falsely weighted upon an order or diligent cause, principle of reality and existence. Thus, *'a priori'*, regardless of what mankind's plans to rest among the stars or even if we cease to exist as a species, the remainder of the universe will remain intact and in existence. It will remain no less evident, the example of clear and distinct perception within discursive reasoning through astute, obscure and uncertain or commandingly clear within the nothingness of life in comparison to the complexity of the cosmos spinning in unison in an instantaneous moment.

To be really distinct, something in the substance and form of a formal train of thought must encompass the habit of self perception contained in the nature or concept. Self evidence in the grandeur of possibility in the reality or perceived reality of, on account of hypotheses, merely to distraction and discursive reasoning inherent and unnecessarily syllogistically synchronous whilst divergent in their perfection. Whatever the idea or questions of perceived reality there is still one awesome truth that outweighs knowledge of all things as viewed even by God. That of time.

However, the first defeat of a non-existent thing where discursive reasoning, logic and contemplation of the nature of the same holds a substance that for some is the normality of routine where only an axiom holds true of a depicted judgement of the existence of time where time is a human conception. Time was designed to describe a definite period identified through standardisation over the ages; until the onception of an idea such as the unit of time expressed in the word 'second' or 'minute', 'hour', 'day', 'month' or 'year'. The senses perceive the certainty of chronological interaction and extension within our given environment such that the astuteness to know anything corporeal, acquired for the habit of perceiving. The note of faith in the sense fails at times such as when the sameness of one item is relative to another item. It is irraational to call into doubt a thing in its very existence except where that alone is necessary in the interests of self preservation observed through a more precise and highly focused substance.

The idea of an infinite particle is a highly complex construction of a term that is more objective in reality as with the idea of a liquid reality for clothes made solely of its core constituents. Contained in the concept of a limited thing, perfection, which can be found lacking due to the limitation of a thing has been replaced with consumption of limited products in heavily stagnated markets.

Distinction of two relative items, objects if you will, requires knowledge of both items such that you only truly need one objects generalised attributes to allow for the provision or negation of truth or falsehood. Perception of all perfections and imperfections of generalised attribution allows for the decision making process to object to the objective reality of one object over another. This is done such that either in the presence of an observer or witness, the subject might affirm or negate perception of a demonstrated object. Whilst a number of attributes can be attributed, surmised from verbal inspection, note on similarity and generalised objectivity such that an objects characteristic likeness might be recognised.

    The power to preserve the perfection I lack is compounded only by all the things I lack in the form of perfection from a generalised point of view. To assume or attribute superiority or apparently inferior forms of existence merely perpetuates the division in which all things cease to be created equal. Despite the falsehood of such a statement as a proposition with no presuppositions preceding. Had I the power to presume to preserve the very essence of my core being where I cease to exist, I find that I am capable of perceiving or conceiving the opposite notion, namely, 'all things are created equal'.

The nature of such statements can be affirmed or negated through observation and observational parallax or perceptual synchronicity. As solitary individuals we perceive substance in so far as a car that is yellow ill remain yellow whether viewed by one person or a multitude in one instant from multiple angles.

Synchronous relative geometrical and metaphysical discourses and discursive reasoning as a form of analysis such as the examples mentioned above in the postulates, axioms and hypotheses are a means with which to extend the same forms subsistence to existence be it temporo-geometric or metaphysical or otherwise.

All of this rests true
based on the following axioms:-

I. To clearly perceive and understand the words 'equality' and 'rights', these are inalienable constructs and indivisible from the person where if one knows and understands something to be a perceptual truth, it becomes their truth. i.e. where no falsehood or inconsistency resides within an ideal as reasoned by a conceptual hypothesis and and ratified by a strong moral countenance, the inalienable and indivisible alike become the perceptual truth or goals(s) to be attained.

II. The corporeal body, mind or soul are distinct

having differing roles within the waking corporeal world with regards to how they interact and perceive objects that cause sensations and emotions.

III. Human cognition requires its substance, the bi-products of thought, for sound and reasoned 'thought'; the attribute with which the mind manifests itself and is to be understood by other well-reasoned minds.

IV. Formal declaration of substance within a forum that is receptive allows for the dissemination of ideas such that they can be shared and understood. Substance, in this very real sense being attributable characteristics of a property, nature or quality of them such that it can be seen to be evident. An example of the same might include the reflection of light; illumination dispenses, as the object of investigation, with the shadows and anything that lacks illumination. Therefore imagine the properties and products of light without a source of emission; the perplexing thought that leads to a mute point, i.e. in the natural world, it is increasingly difficult to find the products of illumination, the very substance of it, without the (a) source of emission.

V. Formal institutions, the dominant objects of our ideas and the route to institutional learning can also be subject to the very same ideas we allow into existence. Being the object of institutional learning as an example of the object of our ideas allows us to perceive the very same ideas through specific lenses such that where there are issues, these can be resolved timeously and without deterrent.

VI. The objective/superlative matrix exists purely in the objects of our ideological fruits, which can be and usually are attuned in line with our shared morals and beliefs. Such is the case that they are indistinguishable from the indiscriminateness of our representative ideas. Once can speak of certain ideas and ideology in the same interchangeable sense. However, without strong moral leadership, direction and command of a breadth of knowledge in order to put an idea into practice, it remains as such.

Objectively, wielding an unseen, or rather, unforeseen idea(s) can be fraught with the same dangers unnecessarily as wielding an unlicensed bi-product of centuries of armed conflict. In opposition to warfare, a solution of ideals is the only route to peace through reasoned and calculated theorem applied. To exist in the object of our desires, thoughts and actions, we must fashion and mould the idea such that it is a societal good and not the evil inherent in mankind. To identify with an image of the mind incompatible with the objective/subjective matrix is near impossible where the mind is inspired by the strong moral conceptions and perceptions of ideas and ideologies that fit the object and (or) subjective will of imagination.

VII. The axiom, perceptual precept or conceptual train of thought both at one and the same time followed by the conscious and subconscious mind is the jewel in the metaphorical crown of the brain at which we find the first vestiges of an idea, a thought and motion rolled into action.

The form with which the idea manifests itself in reality culminates in an instinctual thirst. All this for life, the hegemony of a conceptual precept or inkling of a notion manifest in the motor skills of an individual. Civilisation has long since moved from defining the nature of ideas in favour of mixing and blending old and new ideas and form, substance and immediate perception to create new ideas original. These new ideas contain the images of the brain.

As such we are immediately overcome with sensation; aware of it from the first second as cognition is felt unawares of the tremendous weight of thought. We each perceive the good and evil within society with respect to the attitudes, words and deeds we undertake on a dday to day basis along with the words, thoughts and actions of others. Where other, that is people outside of the self, know intimately and perceive a good moral action, action is then followed with perception to the same.

Most people are able to distinguish the difference between good and evil moral actions. The idea or knowledge of good in the strictest sense separation all things from an object, it would be said to lack the form and substance of the opposite attribute of an object.